CHAINS ARE BROKEN

Epps CreativeMindz Enterprise, LLC
Epps Creativemindz Publishing

Copyright © 2016

All rights reserved. No part of this publication may be reproduced, stored in a retrieval system, or transmitted, in any form, or by any means, electronic, mechanical, photocopying, recording, or otherwise, without the prior consent of the publisher.

**There is Only
One
Direction
"Keep Moving Forward"**

Forward

Life takes one through many transitions and many phases. Sometimes those transitions can be the most elated feelings in the world, and other times it can feel like the lowest most devastating experience of life. What if you were told that both experiences, the highs and the lows were a necessity in life, to help make you a better, more equipped, more efficient and stronger version of yourself? Would you believe it, comprehend it, understand it?

If we only experienced the good in life how would we gain the wisdom from our trials, be inspired from our tribulations, and motivated from our failures to want, have, and do better in life? Jeremiah 29:11 says, "For I know the plans I have for you," declares the Lord, "plans to prosper you and not to harm you, plans to give you hope and a future." God knows that we will have obstacles in life, but he clearly states here that they were sent to develop us for our futures.

Life can throw us many curve balls, and sometimes situations that literally take our breath away, but the one thing that we have is the decision and the determination to say, "I will keep going!"

As you read this inspirational toolkit for your life, you will be motivated, inspired, and gain the wisdom that you need to help you face and maneuver through some of those tough issues of life. Life doesn't stop because difficulties happen. Life keeps going, and so should you. You were created to have life, and have it more abundantly (Ref. John 10:10). Don't be robbed of your inheritance.

Shanitria N. Kittrell
Best Selling Author
Motivational Speaker
Executive Coach

Serenity Prayer

God, grant me the serenity

To accept the things, I cannot change,

Courage to change the things I can,

and wisdom to know the difference.

In Jesus Name Amen

God, give us grace to accept with serenity

the things that cannot be changed,

courage to change the things

which should be changed,

and the wisdom to distinguish

the one from the other.

Living one day at a time,

Enjoying one moment at a time,

Accepting hardship as a pathway to peace,

Taking, as Jesus did,

This sinful world as it is,

Not as I would have it,

Trusting that You will make all things right,

If I surrender to Your will,

So that I may be reasonably happy in this life,

And supremely happy with You forever in the next.

Amen

"If you can't fly then run, if you can't run then walk, if you can't walk then crawl, but whatever you do you have to keep moving forward."

~ Dr. Martin Luther King Jr.

"This world is your best teacher. There is a lesson in everything. There is a lesson in each experience. Learn it and become wise. Every failure is a stepping stone to success. Every difficulty or disappointment is a trial of your faith. Every unpleasant incident or temptation is a test of your inner strength. Therefore, nil desperandum. March forward hero!"

~ Swami Sivananda

Be the Creator of your Destiny; Unveil your Purpose!

-Author DuWanda S. Epps

Don't Quit

When things go wrong as they sometimes will,

When the road you're on seem so far,

When the funds are low and the debts are high

you want to smile, but you have a frown,

When life is pressing you down a bit,

You seem lost or you don't have away.

Life is filled with twists and turns,

As we all know,

many a failure and mistakes

But life is a lesson, so learn from it;

Don't give up even when pace seems slow

You fall but get back up and keep moving,

Success comes when you keep working,

Don't hide when the silver tint clouds are near,

Your faith is being tested and you break through maybe near

So stand firm when things seem at its worst

Be victorious & courageous

Don't Quit!

~ Author DuWanda S. Epps

Happiness keeps you smile,

Trial keeps you strong,

Tears keep you human,

Failures keeps you determined

Success keep you humble

But God keeps you going!

Author DuWanda S. Epps

She is clothed in Strength & Dignity and she laughs

without fear of the Future

Proverbs 31:25

Faith is taking a first step even when you don't see

the whole staircase

"Gratitude unlocks the fullness of life. It turns what we have into enough, and more. It turns denial into acceptance, chaos to order, confusion to clarity. It can turn a meal into a feast, a house into a home, a stranger into a friend. Gratitude makes sense of our past, brings peace for today, and creates a vision for tomorrow."

~ Melody Beattie

Keep Moving Forward

Your pain has a purpose

Roman 5:3-5

The tallest oak in the forest was once just a little nut

that held its ground

To believe a thing is impossible is to make it so

If you want to grow, and you want to change, you must learn to let go of the habits and excuses that's keeping you in the past

You can't be who are going to be, and who you used to be at the same time.

-T D Jakes

I am convinced that life is 10% of what happened to you and 90% how you react to it.

The only thing that hurts harder than a failure is not

trying

-Apoorve Dubey

Limits are only the ones you set for yourself;

You got to Achieve

When you adopt a positive attitude

The key is to always look for the good in any given circumstance

Be ready

Stay Focus

Even through the Storms

Stay hungry & determined

Even when things seem cloudy

Keep You 're eyes on your prize

Be Hungry but Humble

Be observant, be aware of your surroundings

Never give up

Keep going

Take pride in all you do

He who is not courageous enough to take risk will

accomplish nothing in life

-Muhammed Ali
(1942-2016)

You have 100% control over your response to events

in life

CHAINS ARE BROKEN

Live

Life

To

The

Fullest

Don't worry be happy

Don't be can what you don't like

CHAINS ARE BROKEN

Doubt kills more dream than failure

Do the right thing,

in spite of what the other person is doing

"I am the greatest ever. I said that before I knew I was"- Muhammad Ali

Remember how are blessed you are.

Don't take anything for granted

CHAINS ARE BROKEN

Always be proud of who you see when you look in

the mirror

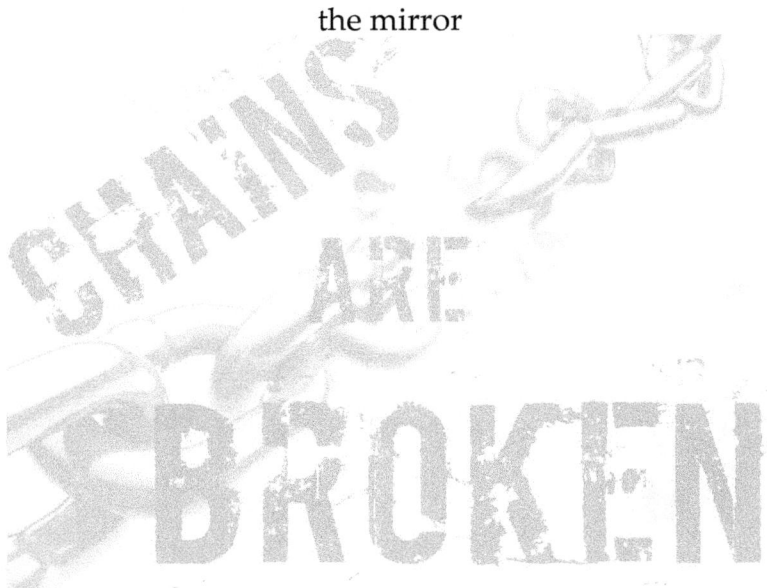

Always walk with your head held high

You can accomplish anything you put your mind too.

Never give up,

something take time;

So be patient and humble.

When a sister fall, her sister will always life her up

Through sisterhood sisters stick together.

Always read the fine,

there holds important information

Silent voices can't be heard

Pay attention to detail

Love yourself first before you can truly love another

If you pay with your life, others will too

Always be true to yourself.

If a person is not true to themselves don't expect them to be true to you.

Worry about nothing and pray about everything.

Beautiful sound better than sexy

Be a positive role model for others.

Leadership defines integrity and character

There is not such word as you can't

No is not final

Power Manifestation of the Universe

Like attracts like

Thoughts creates situations and circumstances:

You get what you think and speak about

You have the capability to bring forth what you want

in your life

Be cautious: Positive thoughts attract positive events

&

Negative thoughts attract negative events

If your feelings and thoughts consist of hardships and

obstacles, then hardship & obstacles will be what you

get

Embrace all the possibilities, keep thinking and expecting success without allowing doubts, you will eventually achieve what seemed impossible

It is not enough just to wish for something, you need strong desire and faith to manifest what you want.

For your thoughts to manifest, you must repeat them often, and add feelings, desire and interest.

Your mind functions like a magnet

Similar energy attracts similar energy

Positive equals Positive

Negative equals Negative

Your thoughts are dormant they

determine the way you live

Law of Attraction is used daily, though mostly unconsciously

Stress kills, filling the mind with worries, toxicants

and anxieties brings stress, unhappiness & death

Filling your mind with happy thoughts and you will

attract happier days to come

Courage is like a muscle

We strengthen it with use

A woman is the full circle.

Within her there is power to create, nurture and the ability to transform.

Love is what we were born with

Fear is what we have learned

No one can make you fear them,

without your consent

No need for a wishbone when you have a backbone

CHAINS ARE BROKEN

The most effective way of doing something,

is to just do it

The secret of getting ahead is getting started

Women are wiser than men because they know less

and understand more

Women have a wonderful instinct about things;

They can discover everything except the obvious

A woman can break down temporarily but she will always pick up the pieces, rebuild herself and come back even stronger than ever

Physical, Verbal, Mental, Financial, Sexual

Are all Abuse

Break free from mental war fare

You can be your worst critic

It's not over because the blood is being applied to

what you are going through

Realize when the times and season are changing

If you have ever been broken,

you are still in the arms of God!

No matter what, people will talk

some are excited that you break free for the warfare.

Some are mad you made it out of the warfare

Never live so desperate that you cling to people that don't want any good for you

Not every place, people or thing is healthy for you

Be careful

You should get beyond the loses in life

To gain happiness

With walls up

You will miss your opportunity

Walls are barriers

Barrier when you have experienced hurt and pain

To be victorious

Your barriers need to be destroyed

Be careful: Don't let your bitterness speak for you

Sometimes there are lesson that must learned in

hardship

How you end is more important than how you begin

You are a choice away from a better life

Make it

Be mindful

Every choice comes with unchosen consequences

Good or Bad

It is possible to have good spiritual grounding and be

a wreck emotionally and physically

Our issues are sent by God to instruct us.

CHAINS ARE BROKEN

Just stay quiet

Sit back and watch the actions of ours

Self-Peace is the Key

Where there is hope there is Faith

Where there is faith Miracles happen

Attract what you expect

Reflect what you desire

Become what you respect

And Mirror what you admire

What Beauty looks like

Encouragement

Acceptance,

Forgivingness and

Compassion

Admire the individuals who choose to shine even after all the storms they've been through

Silence won't ever make a Best Seller

Be a Bald Eagle

Spread your wings

And fly

Don't be angry at all the people who told you No,

Instead thank them because of them you did it by yourself.

Believe in You!!!

If you're feeling like you're in hell

Keep going

Don't give up

You cannot hang out with negative people

and

expect positive

Some people actual only check on you to see if you failed yet!!

Be a Goal Achiever

Instead of

A Gold Digger

A Dream written down with a date becomes a goal.

A goal broken down into steps becomes a plan.

A plan backed by action makes your Dreams

A Plan in Action.

Checklist to Self

- ✓ Keep going
- ✓ Keep praying
- ✓ Stay positive
- ✓ Be determine
- ✓ Be Patient
- ✓ Become an Achiever

Never take someone's feelings for granted because you never know how much courage that they took to show it to you.

Don't look for love

Realize you are worth love looking for you

God all use your deepest pain

To be used as the greatest calling

You fall,

Rise Make mistake,

learn from them

Have confidence

Have faith

Continue putting one foot in front of the other

And continue to move forward

Confidence is beautiful

It does not matter the size, color, sex or age

Be confidence in who you are

And

Trust you are beautiful

Pray for guidance, strength when you feel lost,

confused or alone

He will clear your mind and direct your path

Just ask and believe.

Prayer and Faith

Changes things situations, attitude, people and relationship

God is an Awesome God

His Grace is Bigger than your Sins

CHAINS ARE BROKEN

Be thankful for God not giving up on you when you gave up on yourself

He knows your struggles

CHAINS ARE BROKEN

One kind word can change someone's' entire day

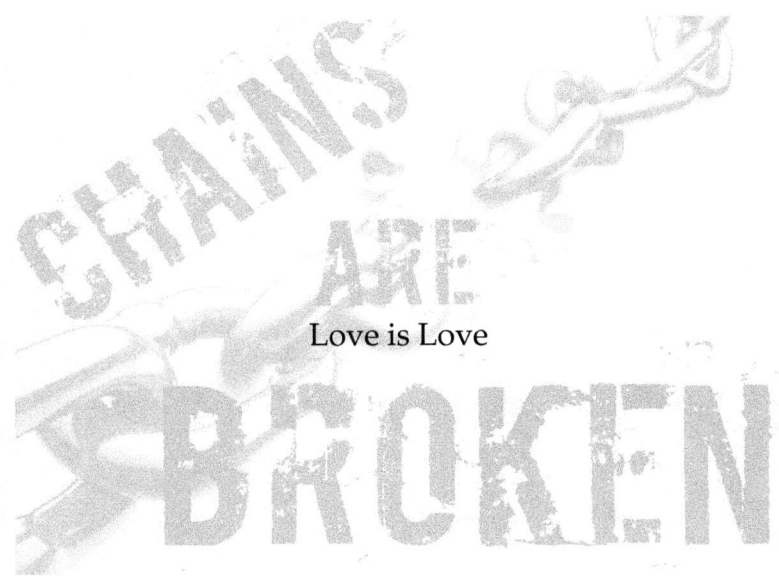

Love is Love

The hardest things in the World is the say "I am

Sorry"

And "I forgive you"

Be careful not to bring baggage to any relationship

CHAINS ARE BROKEN

Baggage only weights you down

Release it

And set yourself free

Faith does not rest in the wisdom of men,

But in the power of God.

1 Corinthians 2:5

Placed in places for a reason, meeting the right people longer than a season.

God can bring peace to your past

Purpose to your present and hope to your future

John 14:27

You're going into a season where you're about to

experience

Breakthrough after breakthrough because what you

went through didn't break you

God is within her she will not fall

Psalm 45:6

Don't have to be sisters by blood to be sister by heart.

Every day is a blessing

Rejoice and be glad in it

CHAINS ARE BROKEN

Rise Up

Get a fresh start

Engage in bright opportunities

Each and Everyday

There is no love without forgiveness

And there is no forgiveness without love

Forgiveness is the key to your freedom

CHAINS ARE BROKEN

There is nothing wrong

with owning up to something when you did wrong

Its shows courage

In life, you have to go through the worst, just to get to

the best

Women were created differently because men can't

adore our pain.

A woman will look like she wasn't crying the night

before

She believed and so she did

I've been knocked down put down and let down so I

know when my sister falls to lift her up

When the road gets though, don't be afraid just

change your shoes

Why play with fire, when all you should

do is put it out.

CHAINS ARE BROKEN

When you do an assessment on individuals around you and if you have a X by their name that affirmation they need to go. X means exit

Discover you own inner strength and take your

power back and make a transformation.

Reaching your goals does not bring happiness, but

the journey you took to get there.

In the mist of pain, later had something worth writing about.

Silence creates a self-made bomb waiting to explode.

With my growth came wisdom and with wisdom

come understanding

Your situation does not determine your final destination

I had made many mistakes to the perfect but I have

too many blessings to be ungrateful.

Success prompts determination and hard work

Success don't embrace laziness or procrastination.

Delegate task to others and manage time wisely

Don't say you can't until you have tried

CHAINS ARE BROKEN

When the Lord speaks listen attentively

If he trying to get you attention, trust he will gain it

another way.

Creative minds don't sleep

Business minded people brain is always working

Art is all shapes and colors joining together

Creativity defines artistic minds and hands at work.

When you find strength from God you remain

faithful and loyal no matter what loss or pain you had

felt.

Pain can promote positive change

#Roc'On#UrWorthy#

It's starts with you!

CHAINS ARE BROKEN

When you receive 1. No, 2. No and even 3. No…

don't give up..

Be humble, Patient and Determine…

The Yes/ Door(s) is about to OPEN!…

Be the Creator of your Destiny; Unveil your Purpose!

-Author DuWanda S. Epps

Sometimes in the mist of pain, it rains to wash away

the pain.

CHAINS ARE BROKEN

Pain brings about positive change.

Pain create preparation for what's to come.

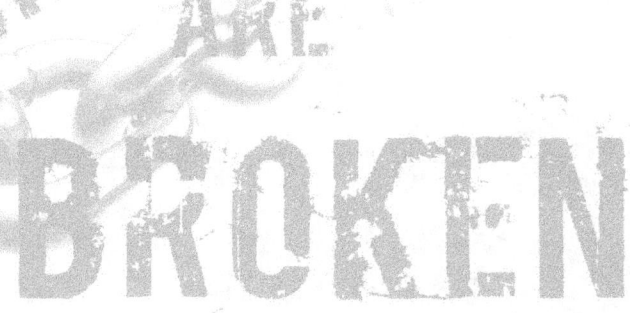

Life is designed to be unseen but the Lord grants us with serenity.

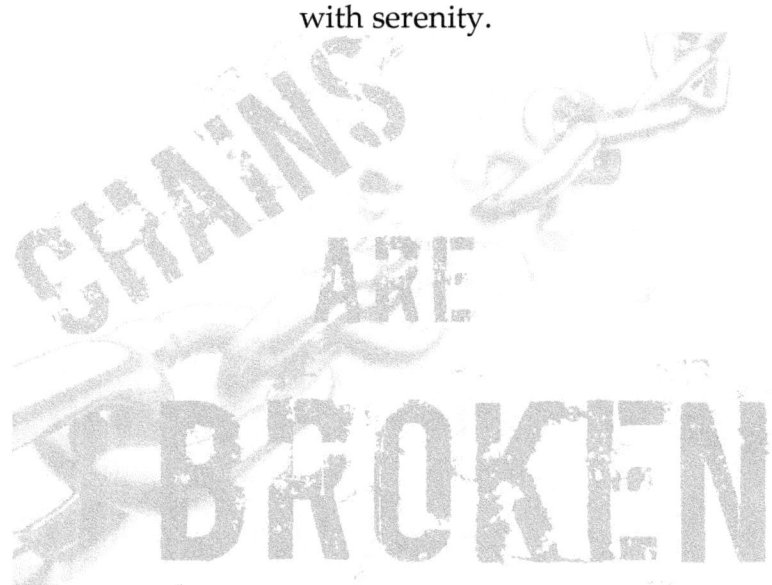

Gods plan isn't our own.

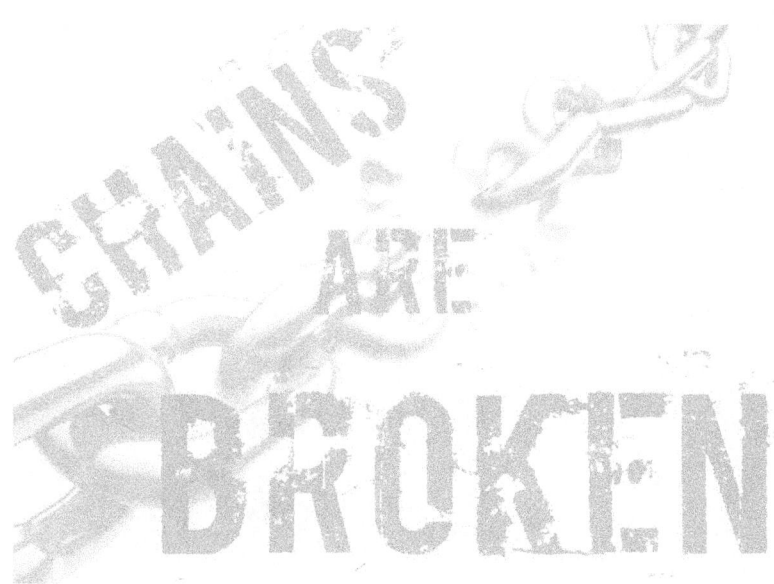

Women were created differently because men can't adore our pain.

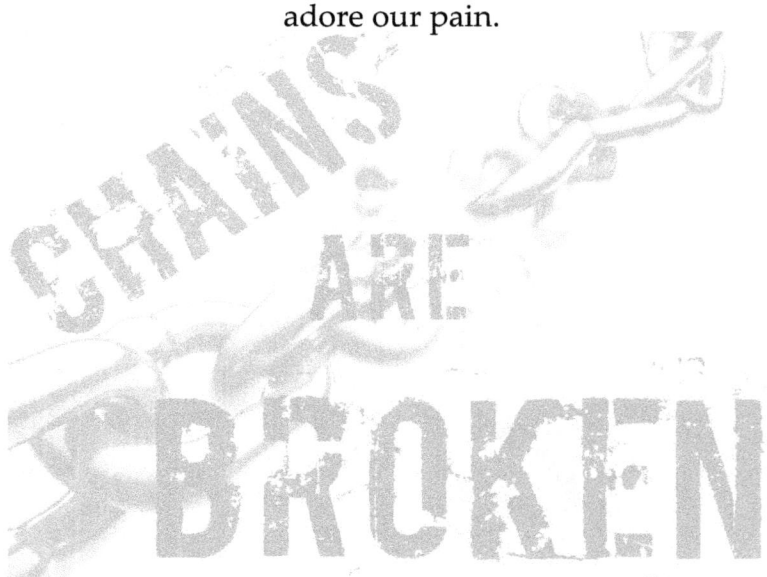

A woman will look like she wasn't crying the night before

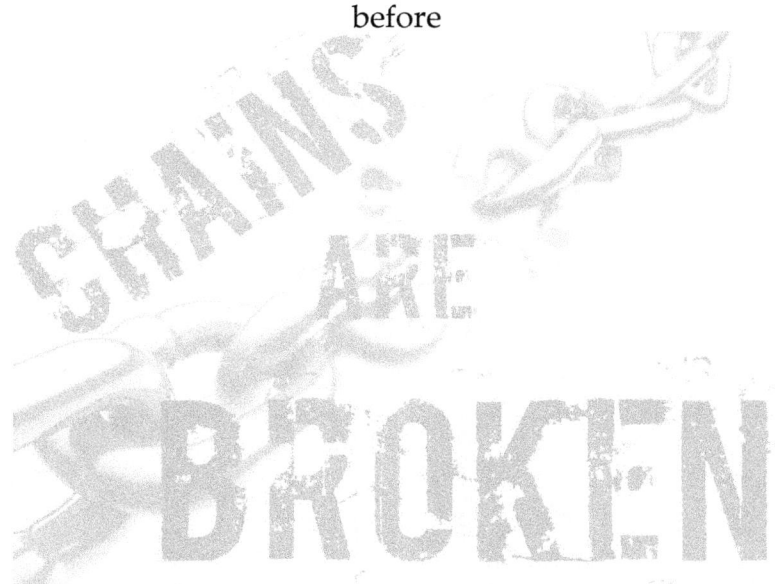

She believed and so she did

CHAINS ARE BROKEN

A woman possesses a lot of power she just let some people borrow it

I am my past; I am my present and proudly I am my future

Love like there is no tomorrow

Blessed, determined, hungry and humble

CHAINS ARE BROKEN

It doesn't make sense now but soon you will know.

Stand firm, be determined and patient humble and blessed.

Women don't earn power; she just takes it!

Another day is a blessing providing opportunity to

change tomorrow

When God has an assignment on your life, you must

complete it!

Treat others the like you want to be treated

A married man or woman

Should be off limits

Have faith small as a mustard seed

There is nothing wrong with hard work

If you don't succeed, try again

CHAINS ARE BROKEN

Prayer answer things

> Maturity
> is not measured by age.
> It's an attitude
> built by experience.

BROKEN

Respect goes a long way

CHAINS ARE BROKEN

Somethings are worth fighting for

Just be smart on what those things are

You can teach a person of know it all already

They are not willing to learn

Times is of the essences

Once it's gone you

Won't get it back

No such thing as catching up on sleep

One hour lost will take 2 days to gain back

Be true to yourself

CHAINS ARE BROKEN

Leopards don't change their spots

Practice safe sex

Saves life's

Have standards

saves a lot of headaches

Only if you allow it

It will happen and/or continue

Your body should be your temple

Treat it as such

Love don't equal to abuse

Any kind of abuse

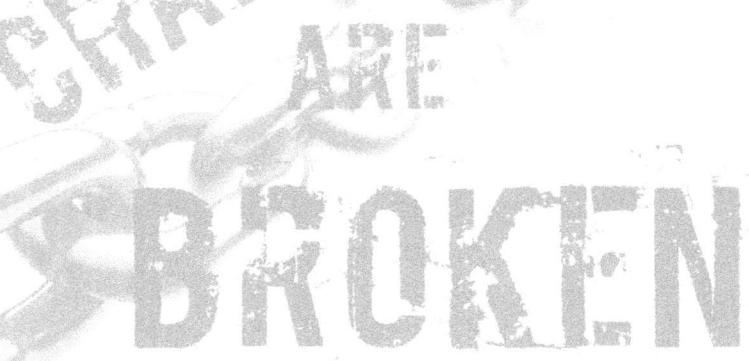

Learn to listen to your body

It speaks truth

Love is gentle and kind

Every day will not be the same

Be your children's first role model

Have morals and values

Never allow yourself to be so desperate that you end up settling for far less than what you deserve.

Drugs Kill

It doesn't solve problems

Only makes them worse

Tears is not a show of fear

Be thankful

For life

Whether the storm

Sunshine will come

Love freely

Time heals old wounds

Because you were hurt in the past

Don't allow that to define your future

Be responsible

Be accountable

For your actions

Trust your gut

Be Bold

Creative

Courageous

Be Beautiful

Attitude can make you or break you

You are capable to change it

Don't depend on others to put a smile on your face!

Not all grass is greener on the other side

CHAINS ARE BROKEN

It's difficult to lie to a lair

Be women of sustains

And

Men of Love

A

Couple of Power!

Let the good times roll

CHAINS ARE BROKEN

Good vibes only

IF YOU CAN'T CHANGE YOUR FATE, CHANGE YOUR ATTITUDE.

Hastag #UrWorthy#Roc'On

CHAINS ARE BROKEN

You got to believe

Eye of the tiger

-Rocky

Make it a habit. See every problem as an opportunity. As you regularly start to look for opportunities in a problem, as you continue to think of finding opportunities you will begin to attract more opportunities.

Steadfast- devoted, loyal to a person & belief

Be all you can be!

Don't let someone become a priority in your life…

When you are just an option in theirs

Situations can **MAKE** you or **BREAK** you!

Forgiveness meads broken wings

Remember broken wings can't fly

"Tough times don't last

Tough people do"

(When I first heard it 1993

NMR)

The way I work says a lot about my character

Three Self-Motivational Competencies:

Achievement Drive: Striving to improve or meet a standard of excellence.

Commitment: Embracing the organization's or groups vision and goals.

Initiative and Optimism: Encourage people to seize opportunities and allow them to take setbacks and obstacles in stride.

When all the other things fade away

CHAINS ARE BROKEN

Think about how you can accomplish your goal.

When you think of possible solutions you force your mind and → subconscious mind to find opportunities that will help you achieve the desired results.

Take different views of the situation. Having looked at the scene from your view, look at it from different perspectives, try each of these views: opportunist; → entrepreneur; dreamer; optimist; child; strategist; → architect.

Until it is only you

When the smoke clears

See Who is still standing

Praise him

Because

He is Worthy

Give him your

Highest

Praise

Who are you?

Look in the mirror ask yourself

Take notice of your weakness

Confess them

People watch and report how you go through your

dark moments

Don't judge a book by its cover

Clarify the story

Before you believe all

you are told

Be careful not to attract

People just like you

Watch how you model yourself!

CHAINS ARE BROKEN

Men know how to approach a woman

It determines how she carry yourself

#FACTS#

Listen to Our Elders

Value

Respect

Appreciate

Them all because if it was not for them

We would not be but where we are

Because they

LABORED FOR US TODAY

You need to connect with the right people

When you're down

When you get to the top

Reach down and pull someone up

Don't be selfish

You can't just be satisfied

You should CONTINUE striding

There are 8 days in a week

The 8th day is called

TO LATE DAY

Change your way of thinking

Change IF to When

Claim it

Don't just settle for a little

God will bless you with a lot

Don't careful how you treat people

Push until something happen

CHAINS ARE BROKEN

"Develop an attitude of gratitude, and give thanks for everything that happens to you, knowing that every step forward is a step toward achieving something bigger and better than your current situation."

~ Brian Tracy

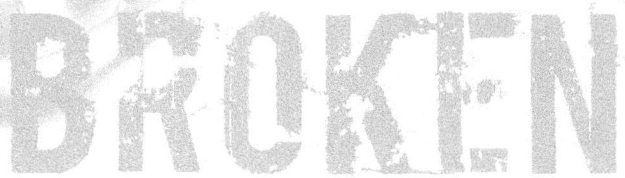

The power has and always will be within you, but nothing will happen until you get and stay motivated to make something happen, to change your life and achieve your desires. Self-motivation empowers you and helps you keep your spirit high no matter how discouraging a situation is.

Change I can't attitude

To

I can

I will

Your attitude can change things

For the better or worse

Shift your focus

Don't focus on the problems, focus on finding opportunities. Don't talk about a problem; talk about an opportunity. When you see a problem as a problem you only attract more problems. If you wish to attract opportunities instead, see the problem as an opportunity. There is an old saying that goes like this: "There are no problems, only opportunities."

Get rid of negative emotions

CHAINS ARE BROKEN

Setbacks are only the opportunity to for a fresh good

Read between the lines

CHAINS ARE BROKEN

Sometimes you need to look through different lens

Take others perspective into consideration

Allow various views to present opportunities.

You should learn something new daily

The brain is like a sponge

Absorb positivity

What may seem to be a failure can lead to new opportunities

Your "I can do it" attitude

Is your successor

To unlocking your future

Seize each opportunity

The worse thing to do is miss it

Or

Mess it up

Capture your moments

CHAINS ARE BROKEN

You hold the power to overcome

Any situation

It's expected to fall

It's unacceptable to fall

And not get backup

Keep pushing

When you treat your problems

Like problems

You create more problems

Food for thought

When you treat your opportunities

Like opportunities

You create more opportunities

positive thoughts generate positive feelings and attract positive life experiences

Bless it be thy name

CHAINS ARE BROKEN

When you have a stink attitude

You stink period.

Instead of fighting

Fire with fire

Fight fire with water

Put it out

Random thoughts are the most creative ones

Unveil your creativity within

CHAINS ARE BROKEN

Choose your battles

Some are not for you to fight

Sharing is caring

Pass it along

When you're at the top

Reach down grab others hand

Can't stop, Won't Stop

Keep on Push

Keep on Striving

Choose to be someone GREAT

The process of healing is to experience pain, then recognition and finally release

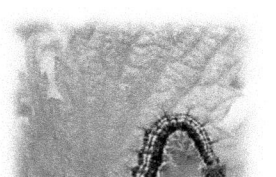

Just when the caterpillar thought the world was

small, it became a butterfly and flew away

When it seems no way

Your Savior will make a way

Stand firm when things seem at its worst

The bravest hearts have the most scars, the courageous actions to still love greatly

Steadfast with your **DREAM**

Don't limit yourself with lack of vision

Always finish what you started

(On the Positive note)

Always believe that something

Wonderful is about to happen regardless of the situation

There is light at the end of the tunnel

BELIEVE IT!!

Imagine with all your mind
Believe with all your heart
Achieve with all your might

International Selling Author DuWanda S. Epps

DuWanda S. Epps, Inspirational Speaker, Therapeutic Mentor, Community Activist, Co-Author of 5, Author of 10 books, including a new-released book, "Tre'Zure Box" (erotica), "Flowin Emotions", "Flowin

Emotions ll" (self-help books). #1 Bestselling author of "Pain 2 Passion: Our Valley Experience" and "Chocolate & Diamonds: Celebrating the Majesty of Motherhood." Featured Guess on The Hotness #1 Online Radio Show- P.O.E.T. (People of Extraordinary Talent) Alabama, Black Satin Radio Poetic Conversations in Ohio and Gee Palace Radio, New York. Rebuilding Broken Lives event in Wilson, NC as an Inspirational Speaker.

Also featured on Magazine Publications and Upcoming interviews with Big Body Casting, June 3rd; Urban Book Authors & Writers of America, 4th edition; DMV, October 2016 edition; Stardom 101 Magazine, July's edition and Authentically You Magazine, May/June 2016 edition. Special guest at

Infinite Entertainment Group, LLC/ Bassment Films Play Irreconcilable Emphasis opening May 21st in Dayton, Ohio. Real Rapp Radio Show on Downtown Hott Radio this June, 2016. Meet the Author September 3rd Urban Moon Book Store.

In addition to upcoming features Author DuWanda S. Epps will be a part of Compilation Book titled Baggage to Blessing and Stories of women of Domestic Violence. Author DuWanda S. Epps is honored to announce her 1st children's book "Friend & Me," cultural diversity, cognitive development reading supporting premature babies and mothers who experienced preeclampsia and dedication to her daughter has a home at Urban Moon Books Store located in Chesapeake, Virginia.

Author DuWanda S. Epps, Graduated of Metropolitan College of New York earned degrees in Human Service, Public Administration. Currently in Graduate program to obtain Doctoral Degree in Public Administration at Capella University. Founder of (EEL) Roc'On Collaborating with fellow Author and Founder of Ur Worthy Movement: Joining together to educate, empower and prevent DV and SA against women and men. Taking courage, strength and faith to take a Stand.

Non for Profit Cultivating Change II, Inc. (2010) assisting families in the community in need of clothing, food, household items and providing resources in the community for additional services and assistance.

- ❖ 3-year recipient of 2014-2015, 2015-2016, 2016-2017 One Warm Coat.
- ❖ 2015 receiver of a letter from Wesley Shelter, Director Mrs. White, Wilson, NC
- ❖ 3 year Adopt a family for Christmas.
- ❖ 15-year List of other asset to the community in the Eastern Carolinas and New York contributions.

Launched of Epps CreativeMindz Enterprise this past Spring 2016. Services include providing reasonable services for small businesses, authors, entertainers and all others with effective marketing and publishing services for their business or brand.

One of the brave women have opened up about their past hurt. Another enlighten, encourage and empowering reading for both men and women globally to show the world that we have turned our pain into #PASSION and #PURPOSE!

Her compassion to serve and service the community for long over a decade. Myself and another Author with the same interest in serving and advocating are initiating a library project for women shelters in our city. Our desire is to provide resilient empowerment stories in the shelters to empower and equip survivors during their transition. To be an empowerment when thoughts are present go to going back to their unhealthy relationships, at this crossroad. Our books can be a pillar to assist them to be strong and help keep them moving in a healthy direction. This project is embraced for My EEL Movement: Enchained (held Captive) *Exculpate (verb Forgive) *Liberate (Freedom).

I am a Survivor!

With compassion to empower, embrace and strengthen women & families for 15 plus years. I am presently a project fund for Women Rebuilding & Transforming to provide 6-12 months of Life Coaching Services FREE to women rebuilding & transitioning in life and/or from battered shelters. My goal is to provide resilient empowerment and supportive outreach to promote self-sufficiency. http://www.plumfund.com/crowdfunding/eel-movement-sister-2-sister

Calling on other Authors who supports taking a stand for DV and SA. To assist our Empowering Library authors must donate (1) book per participating shelter with envisioning recognition in their name.

Upcoming Writing Projects & Opportunities includes these Anthologies:

1. Redefining Sisterhood (2017)

2. Daily Inspirational Devotion (2017)

3. Single Fathers Journey, I have a Heart.

4. Children's Poetry "Rhymes & Reasons (2016)- An young author entrepreneurship opportunity project

Stayed tuned for: *"Broken Silence"*

Short Film/ Documentary

A short film about an African American woman's story of triumph, abuse, and faith. The main character witnesses' domestic violence as a child, then grows up to be in a violent relationship herself. She also experiences sexual abuse as well as being a homeless pregnant teen. Her broken marriage leads to a near drug overdose. Despite the hurt and pain, she was able to graduate high school, college and earn a Master's Degree at the age of 25. A world of struggles did not keep her from being the woman and living the life destined for her.

Broken Silence "Life after the Storm" Stage Play

Fall/Winter 2017

Stay Connected:

www.flowinemotions.weebly.com
www.authordsepps.com
https://www.linkedin.com/in/authordsepps
authordsepps@outlook.com
Twitter: **flowinemotions**
Instagram: **BestSellinAuthorDSE**
www.eppscreativemindzenterprise.com

www.ingramcontent.com/pod-product-compliance
Lightning Source LLC
Chambersburg PA
CBHW070632160426
43194CB00009B/1444